Positive thinking and mindset

Change your thoughts

Jacklyn R Pollard

Table of contents

Introduction

Positive thinking is the practice of focusing on the positive side of things. It's part of positive psychology, and has been increasingly popular since the 1990's.

In fact, the power of positive thinking has been known for millennia. Greek philosophers celebrated the importance of concepts like "eudaimonia" (roughly translated to fulfilment) and hedonic happiness, or subjective well being. And slightly more recently, Thomas Jefferson advised to "Take things always by their smooth handle".

For example, positive thinking has been shown to have a host of physical benefits. It is known to improve physical health and longevity, and to reduce blood-pressure and stress. It also reduces the risk of heart attacks and increases resistance to illnesses like the common cold.

Positive thinking also changes the way we think. This can lead to benefits for individuals and teams in the world of work. For example, positive thinking leads to increased clarity of thinking, creativity and problem solving. It also helps people manage their mood more effectively, and improve their coping skills.

Chapter 1
What is positive thinking and mindset

What is positive thinking
Positive thinking means approaching life's challenges with a positive outlook.
 It doesn't mean seeing the world through rose-coloured lenses by ignoring or glossing over the negative aspects of life.
Positive thinking does not necessarily mean avoiding difficult situations. Instead, positive thinking means making the most of potential obstacles, trying to see the best in other people, and viewing yourself and your abilities in a positive light.

Optimistic explanatory style: People with an optimistic explanatory style tend to give themselves credit when good things happen and typically blame outside forces for bad outcomes. They also tend to see negative events as temporary and atypical.
Pessimistic explanatory style: People with a pessimistic explanatory style often blame

themselves when bad things happen, but fail to give themselves adequate credit for successful outcomes. They also have a tendency to view negative events as expected and lasting. As you can imagine, blaming yourself for events outside of your control or viewing these unfortunate events as a persistent part of your life can have a detrimental impact on your state of mind. Positive thinkers are more apt to use an optimistic explanatory style, but the way in which people attribute events can also vary depending upon the exact situation. For example, a person who is generally a positive thinker might use a more pessimistic explanatory style in particularly challenging situations, such as at work or at school.

Do you tend to see the glass as half empty or half full? You have probably heard that question plenty of times. Your answer relates directly to the concept of positive thinking and whether you have a positive or negative outlook on life. Positive thinking plays an important role in positive psychology, a subfield devoted to the study of what makes people happy and fulfilled.

Research has found that positive thinking can aid in stress management and even plays an important role in your overall health and well-being.1 It can help combat feelings of low self-esteem, improve physical health, and help brighten your overall outlook .

Note:
While there are many factors that determine whether a person has a positive outlook, the way that they explain the events of their life, known as their explanatory style, plays an important role.

Positive Psychology vs. Positive Thinking
While the terms "positive thinking" and "positive psychology" are sometimes used interchangeably, it is important to understand that they are not the same thing. Positive thinking is about looking at things from a

positive point of view. It is a type of thinking that focuses on maintaining a positive, optimistic attitude. Positive psychology is a branch of psychology that studies the effects of optimism, what causes it, and when it is best utilised.

Health Benefits of Positive Thinking
In recent years, the so-called "power of positive thinking" has gained a great deal of attention thanks to self-help books such as "The Secret." While these pop-psychology books often tout positive thinking or philosophies like the law of attraction as a sort of psychological panacea, empirical research has found that there are many very real health benefits linked to positive thinking and optimistic attitudes.

Positive thinking is linked to a wide range of health benefits, including:
Better stress management and coping skills
Enhanced psychological health
Greater resistance to the common cold
Increased physical well-being
Longer life span

Lower rates of depression
Reduced risk of cardiovascular disease-related
death

One theory is that people who think positively
tend to be less affected by stress. Research
suggests that having more positive automatic
thoughts helps people become more resilient in
the face of life's stressful events. People who had
high levels of positive thinking were more likely
to walk away from stressful life events with a
higher sense of the meaningfulness of life.
Another possibility is that people who think
positively tend to live healthier lives in general;
they may exercise more, follow a more
nutritious diet, and avoid unhealthy behaviours.

How to Practise Positive Thinking
While you might be more prone to negative
thinking, there are strategies that you can use to
become a more positive thinker. Practising these
strategies regularly can help you get in the habit
of maintaining a more positive outlook on life.

Notice your thoughts: Start paying attention to the type of thoughts you have each day. If you notice that many of them are negative, make a conscious effort to reframe how you are thinking in a more positive way.

Write in a gratitude journal: Practising gratitude can have a range of positive benefits and it can help you learn to develop a better outlook. Experiencing grateful thoughts helps people to feel more optimistic.

Use positive self-talk: How you talk to yourself can play an important role in shaping your outlook. Studies have shown that shifting to more positive self-talk can have a positive impact on your emotions and how you respond to stress.

Potential Pitfalls of Positive Thinking
While there are many benefits to thinking positively, there are actually times when more realistic thinking is more advantageous. For example, in some situations, negative thinking can actually lead to more accurate decisions and outcomes.

Some research has found that negative thinking
and moods can actually help people make better,
more accurate judgments.

However, research suggests that realistic
optimism might be the ideal. The results of a
2020 study published in the Personality and
Social Psychology Bulletin revealed that people
who have mistaken expectations, whether those
expectations are optimistic or pessimistic, tend
to fare worse in terms of mental health when
compared to realists

The authors of the study suggest that the
disappointment that optimists experience when
their high hopes are not realised can have a
negative impact on well-being. This doesn't
mean that people should strive to be pessimistic
thinkers. since studies indicate that people with a
negative outlook tend to fare the worst. Instead,
having a generally positive outlook that is
focused on realistic expectations may be the best
approach.

In some cases, inappropriately applied positive thinking can cross the line into what is known as toxic positivity . This involves insisting on maintaining a positive mindset no matter how upsetting, dire, or damaging a situation might be. This type of excessive positivity can impede authentic communication and cause people to experience feelings of shame or guilt if they struggle to maintain such an overly positive outlook.

Note: Positive thinking can have pitfalls at times. While it is important to have an overall positive outlook, unrealistically high expectations can lead to disappointment. Being unable to accept any negative emotions, known as toxic positivity, can also have a negative effect on mental

Positive
 thinking actually means approaching life's challenges with a positive outlook. It does not necessarily mean avoiding or ignoring the bad things; instead, it involves making the most of

the potentially bad situations, trying to see the best in other people, and viewing yourself and your abilities in a positive light.

We can extrapolate from these definitions and come up with a good description of a positive mindset as the tendency to focus on the bright side, expect positive results, and approach challenges with a positive outlook.

Having a positive mindset means making positive thinking a habit, continually searching for the silver lining and making the best out of any situation you find yourself in.

Characteristics and Traits of a Positive Mindset:
6 Examples
-Motivating those around you with a positive word.
-Using the power of a smile to reverse the tone of a situation.
-Being friendly to those you don't know.

-It's getting back up when you fall down. (No matter how many times you fall down.)
-Being a source of energy that lifts those around you.
-Understanding that relationships are more important than material things.
-Being happy even when you have little.
-Having a good time even when you are losing.
-Being happy for someone else's success.
-Having a positive future vision, no matter how bad your current circumstances.
-Smiling.
-Paying a compliment, even to a total stranger.
-Tell someone you know that they did a great job. (And mean it.)
-Making someone's day. (Not just a child's… adult's like to have their day be special, too!)
-It's not complaining no matter how unfair things appear to be. (It is a waste of time… instead, do something!)
-Not letting other people's negativity bring you down.
-Giving more than you expect to get in return.
-Being true to yourself… always

*Why is a Positive Attitude Considered the Key to
Success?*
they come.

Above all, it's about increasing your control over
your own attitude in the face of whatever comes
your way. You cannot control your mood, and
you cannot always control the thoughts that pop
into your head, but you can choose how you
handle them.

When you choose to give in to the negativity,
pessimism, and doom-and-gloom view of the
world, you are not only submitting to a loss of
control and potentially wallowing in
unhappiness—you are missing out on an
important opportunity for growth and
development.

According to positive psychologist Barbara
Fredrickson, negative thinking, and negative
emotions have their place: they allow you to
sharpen your focus on dangers, threats, and

vulnerabilities. This is vital for survival,
although perhaps not as much as it was for our
ancestors.

On the other hand, positive thinking and positive
emotions "broaden and build" our resources and
skills, and open us up to possibilities
(Fredrickson, 2004).

Building a positive framework for your thoughts
is not about being bubbly and annoyingly
cheerful, but making an investment in yourself
and your future. It's okay to feel down or think
pessimistically sometimes, but choosing to
respond with optimism, resilience, and gratitude
will benefit you far more in the long run

mental state, and maintaining a positive attitude
will help patients reduce their tension, anxiety,
fatigue, and depression, and improve their
overall quality of life (Spiegel et al., 2007).

Chapter 2
Two major types of mindset

What Is a Mindset?

Your mindset is a set of beliefs that shape how you make sense of the world and yourself. It influences how you think, feel, and behave in any given situation. It means that what you believe about yourself impacts your success or failure.

According to Stanford psychologist Carol Dweck, your beliefs play a pivotal role in what you want and whether you achieve it.1 Dweck has found that it is your mindset that plays a significant role in determining achievement and success.

Mindsets can influence how people behave in a wide range of situations in life. For example, as people encounter different situations, their mind triggers a specific mindset that then directly impacts their behaviour in that situation.

Fixed vs. Growth Mindsets

According to Dweck, there are two basic mindsets: fixed and growth. If you have a fixed mindset, you believe your abilities are fixed traits and therefore can't be changed. You may also believe that your talent and intelligence alone lead to success, and effort is not required.

On the flip side, if you have a growth mindset, you believe that your talents and abilities can be developed over time through effort and persistence. People with this mindset don't necessarily believe that everyone can become Einstein or Mozart just because they try. They do, however, believe that everyone can get smarter or more talented if they work at it.

Here are some fixed vs. growth mindset examples.
Fixed Mindset vs Growth Mindset
Either I'm good at it or I'm not. I can learn to do anything I want.
That's just who I am. I can't change it. I'm a constantly evolving work in progress.

If you have to work hard, you don't have the ability.The more you challenge yourself, the smarter you become.

If I don't try, then I won't fail.I only fail when I stop trying.

That job position is totally out of my league.

That job position looks challenging. Let me apply for it.

How Mindset Forms

So how is your mindset created in the first place? Dweck's research reveals two primary sources: praising and labelling, both of which occur in early childhood.

The Impact of Praise

In a landmark series of experiments, Dweck and her colleagues found that kids behaved very differently depending on the type of praise they received.2 They found that personal praise, or praising a child's talents or labelling them as "smart," promotes a fixed mindset. It sends a message to a child that they either have an ability or they don't, and that there is nothing they can do to change that fact.

Process praise, on the other hand, emphasises the effort a person puts in to accomplish a task. It implies their success is due to the effort and the strategy they used, both of which they can control and improve over time.

Here's an example of how they're different. If your child gets a good grade on a maths test, personal praise might be, "See, you are good at maths. You got an A on your test." Process praise, on the other hand, might sound like this: "I'm impressed by how hard you studied for your maths test. You read the material over several times, asked your teacher to help you figure out the tricky problems, and tested yourself on it. That really worked!"
What are the two types of mindset?
Mindset develops early in one's life. Experts think that mindset is a combination of experiences, values, and how children are raised. While each individual's mindset is unique, they

can be grouped into two general types: fixed mindset and growth mindset (O'Keefe et al., 2018).

Fixed Mindset
Fixed mindset refers to the belief that ability or talent are fixed traits that do not change over time (O'Keefe et al., 2018). It sees effort as bad as one should not have to work hard if they have the talent or skill. Those with such a mindset are concerned with the appearance of being smart to prove their abilities.

Individuals who are taught to have this behaviour are focused on how they are judged. Consequently, a fear of not living up to expectations develops during early childhood. Furthermore, they see helplessness as a sign of failure, which means it is time to give up.

Growth Mindset
People with a growth mindset consider abilities as malleable. As such, they believe that talent is developed over time through practice, studies,

and other endeavours. They enjoy challenges and are more likely to explore and embrace new experiences.

Instead of considering mistakes as the end, they see it as an opportunity to try new approaches. They are open to making errors for the sake of learning. This means they develop resilience and grit during their formative years. Students with a growth mindset have greater chances of thriving in many challenging circumstances. For example, online college students with a growth mindset will actively seek opportunities to socialise and make friends regardless of their unique academic set-up.

brain's ability to reorganise and remodel to adapt to new situations and changes in the environment (Demarin & Morović, 2014).

The brain is likened to a malleable plastic. It continues to develop throughout one's lifetime, even during adulthood. It reshapes itself as it creates and loses neural pathways.

A key component of a growth mindset is motivation, which can be traced to certain parts of the brain, such as the ventral striatum and anterior cingulate cortex (Ng, 2018). Motivated behaviours directly affect people's thoughts and actions.

As students focus more on learning, neural pathways are established. Practising skills leads to the formation of more neuronal circuits that leads to better ability in performing particular tasks. The brain becomes familiar with these pathways, thereby further developing the ability until it becomes "easy" to the individual.

As these thoughts and actions become a habit, it becomes "hardwired" to the brain. The repetition of tasks creates "routes" that become easier to use.

For example, solving mathematical problems creates millions of neural pathways. In the beginning, solving such problems is more difficult as the circuits are not fully developed. However, as the student continues to practise and learns from mistakes, new connections are created each time, which leads to better critical and logical thinking.

How to Develop a Growth Mindset?
Mindset development primarily happens during childhood, which means parents, teachers, and peers have a significant effect on one's attitude towards ability (O'Keefe et al., 2018). However, this does not mean that students cannot develop a growth mindset on their own. There are numerous steps that help develop a growth mindset (Briggs, 2020).

First, acknowledging one's imperfections is an excellent start, especially in recognizing challenges and failures as opportunities for self-improvement. Additionally, it shifts the focus on learning instead of seeking approval. Different learning tactics can be explored to further improve one's ability by focusing on the process instead of the end result.

As the ability of an individual to appreciate learning and development improves, it becomes easy to cultivate a sense of purpose by setting goals that celebrate growth instead of speed. Valuing growth allows an individual to accept criticism as a necessary element of improvement.

Developing a growth mindset is a continuous process. Just like what the mindset entails, its development requires an effort that highlights one's ability to improve over time.

Growth Mindset Examples

Sometimes it can be hard to see how a growth mindset can help us be happier and reach our goals. Here are some growth mindset examples to give you more insight.

Henry failed his maths test. Instead of thinking he's not smart, he sees this experience as an indication that he needs to study harder.

Da'Sean wants to change jobs but he will need to be a great public speaker to get the job he wants. But this is no worry to him because Da'Sean knows that he can go to toastmasters and practise public speaking until he gets good enough to get the new job.

Carla has just lost 100 lbs and wants to see the view from the top of a 14er (a mountain 14,000 feet above sea level). She is scared because she has never done anything like this before. But now that she has lost all the weight, she knows that she can do anything. So she goes for small hikes, then larger ones, and in a year, she makes it to the top of a 14er.

Fixed vs Growth Mindset
Carol Dweck, the leading growth mindset researcher, suggests that fixed vs growth mindsets result in us living by different self-implemented rules (Dweck, 2009).

Rule #1
Those with a fixed mindset strive to look talented to others. Those with a growth mindset strive to learn.

Rule #2

Those with a fixed mindset believe they shouldn't work too hard. In fact, having to work hard must mean you're not talented. Carol Dweck suggests this may be because fixed mindset individuals were naturally good at things when they were young. They didn't have to work as hard so later in life when they reach their natural limits, they have a harder time pushing through them.

Those with a growth mindset believe in working with passion and dedication, always striving to give their best effort. These individuals may have had to struggle and work hard for success. As a result, they learned that their efforts really do matter and that they can improve their skills.

Rule #3

Those with a fixed mindset believe they shouldn't attempt things they might fail at and they hide their weakness from others. Those with a growth mindset are not afraid of failure and aim to improve upon their weaknesses even if they look silly or stupid in the process.

Remember though, virtually no one has a 100% fixed or growth mindset. We likely have some aspects of each and we benefit from trying to move more towards the growth mindset side of the continuum.

A positive mindset can be great for our well-being and even help us to be more successful. In fact, the broaden and build theory of positive emotion suggests that positive emotions build on themselves, eventually leading to things like professional and relationship success (Fredrickson, 2004).

Positive Mindset Examples
Greg decides he wants to start a business that one day makes a million dollars. He's optimistic about the likelihood of success.
Arjun completely bombs an assignment at work. But he looks at the experience as a positive because he's grateful to have a job that

challenges him and glad to have the opportunity to try something new.

Elaine's job can be dull. But she doesn't see it that way. She finds ways to make it fun and do nice things for her coworkers, which makes her happy.

When it comes to developing beneficial mindsets there are lots to choose from. Building a little bit of any of these mindsets can help you get on track towards achieving your goals and living the life you want.

Chapter 3
Curbing every negative thoughts

HOW TO CURB NEGATIVE THINKING AND RETRAIN YOUR BRAIN

Although it is normal to have negative thoughts, regularly engaging in negative thinking patterns can be problematic. Negative thinking patterns, also known as cognitive distortions, can have a negative impact on mental health, and although it may be challenging to always remain positive, it is important to work on viewing life through a more positive lens. This post will further explain what cognitive distortions are and provide actionable tips for curbing negative thinking patterns.

WHAT ARE COGNITIVE DISTORTIONS?

Cognitive distortions are thoughts that cause individuals to inaccurately view reality and can lead to worsening negative emotions, anxiety, and depression. The way you communicate with yourself can have a significant impact on your mental health

the following 10 common cognitive distortions:
-Personalization and Blame: You feel responsible for everything and even blame oneself for events that you have no control over. E.g., My child had a bad day at school today because I'm a bad parent.
-Mental Filter: You focus on a single negative detail of a situation. E.g., My co-worker left during my presentation, so it must have been awful.
-Emotional Reasoning: You assume that something is true based solely on the way you feel. E.g., I didn't get the promotion and feel hopeless, so things must really really be hopeless.
-Overgeneralization: You apply the result of a single negative experience to all related experiences. E.g., I was broken up with in the past, so my current partner will also eventually leave me.
-All-or-Nothing Thinking: When an individual sees a situation as either bad or good, with no

middle ground. E.g, I didn't get the exact job offer I wanted, so it's a bad offer.

-Discounting the Positive: You reject or minimise the positive aspects of situations. E.g., I'm a failure, because I only ran 2 miles today instead of 3 like I had planned.

-Jumping to Conclusions: Without sufficient information, you conclude how a situation will play out or how someone else feels. E.g. My friend didn't say bye to me before she left so obviously she is mad at me.

-Magnification/Minimization: You exaggerate or shrink the importance of something. E.g., I got straight A's because the semester was very easy.
-Should statements: You criticise yourself or others using "should statements." E.g. I should have prepared more for the presentation.
-Labelling: You assign a label to yourself or others based on an event or characteristic. E.g. She didn't want to go out with me again because I am a loser.

HOW TO RETRAIN YOUR BRAIN

Fortunately, there are a number of ways you can fight back against negative thinking patterns, and retrain your brain to think more positively. Becoming more aware of your thoughts, learning how to turn negatives into positives, and focusing on self-care can help curb negative thoughts and improve mental health.

1. BE COGNIZANT OF YOUR THOUGHTS

An emotional response is created after an event is interpreted, judged, and . Often, this process involves self-talk and automatic thoughts that we accept as fact. It's important to know that thoughts are not factual statements, they are electrochemical impulses in the brain meant to help us interpret the world around us. However, sometimes they are truly the opposite of helpful.

For example, consider a situation where two individuals are given a promotion.

One person might think, "This is great! I am finally being rewarded for my hard work!", whereas the other person thinks, "They feel sorry for me so they are handing me this opportunity."

These two interpretations or thoughts create vastly different feelings even though the event is exactly the same.

Cognitive Behavioral Therapy (CBT), a type of psychological treatment, tells us that what we think and do significantly affects the way we feel. In order to feel better, we must be open to changing what we think and do. CBT can help people identify and change harmful thinking and behaviour patterns by having individuals examine and understand their beliefs. This type of therapy can really help people understand why they are interpreting the world in a certain way and start to reframe their perspective.

2. TURN NEGATIVES INTO POSITIVES
We all know the saying, "When life gives you lemons, make lemonade." The phrase is meant to inspire optimism, which may be beneficial to individuals. Positive, optimistic thinking can lead to improved physical and mental health. The

Mayo Clinic explains that a positive outlook may enable individuals to cope better with stressful situations, which ultimately reduces the mental and physical toll of stress on the body.

Challenging your inner critic, and changing your thoughts and outlook from a more negative, pessimistic perspective to a more positive, optimistic takes practice, willingness, and openness.

Try to evaluate your thoughts, understand where they are coming from, and find a way to put a more positive spin on any thoughts that are negative.

For example, if you are considering going back to school, but then immediately tell yourself that it's too much work, instead try telling yourself that you are ready to rise to the challenge.

Negative thoughts can have such a profound impact on our wellbeing, so it is critical to work on interpreting and processing information in a more positive way.

3. DEVELOP HEALTHY PRACTICES

Developing a routine, particularly a morning routine, can improve mental health. Consider starting off your day doing something you love or committing to a healthy practice such as meditation, mindfulness, yoga or journaling.

Meditation can assist you in clearing out mental clutter, as well as helping you get in touch with yourself, and mindfulness can help you focus on the present moment.

Consider finding a mantra or meaningful phrase you can repeat. A mantra can also help you feel more connected with your work.

Adding yoga to your morning or daily routine can also help you curb negative self-talk. Additionally, since yoga is a form of exercise, it has additional health benefits such as, increasing endurance and physical strength.

Finally, practising self-reflection can help you develop emotional intelligence, increase confidence, and understand your strengths and weaknesses. Paying attention to the way you think, feel, and behave can be enormously beneficial. This self-awareness technique can help you look at yourself more objectively and better identify your passions, motivations, and purpose.

What Effect Does Negative Thinking Have on Health?

As human beings, we have something in common that is integral to our brain's work. We have thoughts all day long. This is what is commonly referred to as our inner voice.
Inner voices can be filled with affirmations like "I am strong, I am smart, I am kind."
Conversely, our inner voice could be filled with damaging thoughts. Thoughts like "I am weak, I am stupid, I am an embarrassment.". Although we may not always have a positive outlook, we don't always have to suffer from a negative one, either.

The good news is that our willpower and brains can control our thoughts, inner voices, and self-talk. It may take some practice, but combating negative thoughts is paramount for success and good health

What is considered negative thinking?
Negative thinking is a thought process where someone finds the worst in every situation or event. When someone is experiencing negative thoughts, they may turn those thoughts onto themselves or think about others.
An example of negative thinking is, "Dogs could be great companions and brighten things up if they didn't make such a mess and all that noise.". Negative thinking patterns develop easily if not quickly addressed.

Negative thinking vs. negative self-talk
Negative thinking and negative self-talk are similar but differ in a small way. Negative thinking is a blanket statement that covers all aspects of life.

Negative self-talk is when someone puts themselves down inside their head or even out loud to themselves or others. An example of negative self-talk would be "I hate myself because I never get anything right." or "I am so ugly. That's why nobody loves me."

How does negative thinking affect mental health?
Our brain is the most powerful organ in our whole body. So, our thoughts have a huge impact on our health, both mentally and physically.

Physical health consequences of negative thinking
Negative thinking and self-talk can affect the body and physical health in many ways. One of the most notable ways negative thinking affects

our body is by creating chronic stress, which wreaks havoc on our physical health. Chronic stress can deplete the brain chemicals required for happiness. It can also damage the immune system and even upset the hormonal balance of the body.

When someone experiences more negative thinking than positive thinking, it can cause many other health risks.

Some examples of other health risks are:
A greater risk of dementia
Higher risk for stroke
Higher blood pressure
Type-2 diabetes
Uncontrollable inflammation
How can I stop negative thinking?
We must first understand what happens when we think negatively to stop negative thinking. Unfortunately, negative thinking can become habitual, making it difficult to stop. That isn't to say it's impossible, though. It's quite possible,

and the pattern can be changed to turn negative thoughts into positive thoughts.

When breaking a habit, it's important not to get discouraged. Habits happen in cycles. First, a reminder strikes a cue for the thought. Then, performing the thought brings a reward. That reward reinforces the desire to continue the thought. The cycle is never-ending. Until you decide enough is enough.

By enacting small changes, big things can happen.

Here are some actionable ways to turn that negative thinking into positive thinking:

Start using a journal. Write down every time you have a negative thought. Then next to it, write down the opposite of that thought and say it out loud. Doing this in your daily life could have amazing outcomes.

When you realise you are thinking negatively, say "Stop." out loud. It will stop your thoughts directly in their tracks.

Create a bullet list of positive things you can say to yourself. If you catch a negative thought and tell yourself out loud to "Stop," you can then say one of your reminders.

Talk to someone. Have an accountability partner. It can be a friend, a parent, or mental health professional. Explain your negative thoughts. Ask for them to check in on your thought patterns.

Sometimes, we can not change our negative thought patterns alone. This could be due to an underlying mental illness, an addiction, or just not having the proper tools to care for ourselves in this way. There are many ways for you to get help if you need it.

What if I need more help to change my habits?
Getting help to change your thinking may seem extreme. However, it's probably one of the most loving things you can do for yourself. You can show yourself how much you care about your

health by calling the admissions team at Absolute Awakenings.

Absolute Awakenings has many different ways to enhance your mental health. Between behavioural therapy, stress management, strategic application of self-care, group therapy, prescribed medication, and many other modalities, there is a plan that can help you achieve your goals.

Challenge Negative Thoughts
Once we have developed the ability to identify
and name some of our negative thoughts and
thinking traps, we can start to challenge them.
When we have a thought we should ask
ourselves is it: helpful to us, is it evidence based
and is it logical. If it is all of these things, then
great. If it's not all three, then it may be negative
and we might want to challenge it.

Where we think a thought is negative, we should
look to change it or replace it with a positive
thought. We should find thoughts that are
helpful, logical and evidence based and hold on
to them. One way we can challenge negative
thoughts is by coming up with new, positive
thoughts. Our post on the ETC self-coaching
model talks through how to do this in more
detail.

Remember, just because you think something,
doesn't mean you need to believe it.

Use Positive Language and Words

Another way we can challenge negativity is through the words we use. As we allude elsewhere, naming things and using words is very powerful. We can challenge the words that we use and replace potentially negative ones with more positive ones. For example "I have to" is a constricting, negative statement. Whereas, "I want to" is similar in meaning most of the time, but is positive and contains agency. If we can change our language in this way, we'll become more positive.

Similarly, another way we can change our thoughts is by reframing our negative thoughts in more helpful, positive ways. For example, we might re-frame our anxiety as excitement, which is a more helpful thought process. You can learn more about this in our post on reversal theory.

It's not just emotions we can do this with, we can also re-frame our perspectives on many situations we find ourselves in in our lives and in the world of work.
Boost Positive Thinking

We can also apply our attention in such a way that we spend more time and energy on positive things, which boosts our positive thinking. Since the brain can in some ways be trained like a muscle, the more we use certain parts of it, the better we get at them. This is the case with positivity. The more we look for the positive, the more easily we'll find it.

Some things we can do to help increase our attention on the positive include:

Focusing on good things and savouring positive moments,
Practising gratitude and saying thank you more often to people,
Keeping a journal of positive events and celebrating your successes,
Letting more humour into your life and work,
Consciously practising positive self-talk, and
Being in the present, perhaps through meditation, even for just 2 mins a day

Conclusion

Change your thoughts and you change your world.'
So there you have it; the single most effective way to improve your life is to think positively. And yet, if it's that simple, did you really need to read a whole book about it? Well, yes. Because now, having read this book, you'll find it easier to be a positive thinker. You'll now understand

what positive thinking is and what it is not.
You'll know how you can move from negative
thinking to positive thinking and follow up your
positive thoughts with positive action. You'll
also know how to train your brain to think in
positive ways and you'll understand the
difference that positive thinking can make when
you're going through difficult and tough times